BE THE VINTNER!

Manage to be the
Vintner of your Workplace

BE THE VINTNER!

Manage to be the
Vintner of your Workplace

Tamara Jahelka

DEDICATION

To all of the employers and leaders that
I have had the pleasure of working with.

Your professional struggles and pleasures,
as well as my own, have inspired me to write this book.

I hope the parallels bring a smile and cheers.

CONTENTS

PREFACE

For those of you who feel like your company and employees are driving you to drink, read on. While on hiatus after twenty-plus years of working in management and human resources, I am finally ready to put pen to paper and share a revelation that came to me at a winery over a decade ago. I was sipping a glass of wine, and noticed a poster identifying the personalities of grapes. Immediately, I saw a correlation between these grapes and the personalities of several employees. The more I contemplated the notion, the more I realized that not only the personalities of grapes, but the entire process of growing, harvesting, and winemaking had several parallels to managing people. As a result of that day, the seed of this book was planted.

This is not your typical management book, suggesting this or that way to manage your people and create the perfect environment for your organization. Instead, it will vicariously help you to "be the vintner."

You will see opportunities for managing people in a more inspired way. This book infuses passion into management via the behaviors and habits of the vintner. It stimulates your imagination, and helps you to alter your perception of management. Join me in the entertaining concept of being the vintner of your workplace.

INTRODUCTION

The average American employee spends forty-seven hours (the equivalent of six days) per week working, and receives as few as ten days of vacation. In reality, many receive even less vacation, and work many more hours. Because we desire balance in our lives, we resent the personal sacrifices made for our jobs. Ultimately, we hold employers and employees accountable for our work-related suffering.

Thirty years ago, companies invested in employees and committed to lifelong careers that included apprenticeships, benefits, and retirement plans. Employees patiently climbed the corporate ladder, gradually gaining tenure. They were more content, because they felt safe—as though they were investing in their own futures. The end result was trust, pride, and loyalty in employment.

After the downsizing and reengineering movement of the 1980s and the recession of 2008, we have seen tenure shrink and loyalty fade. This shift was initiated by employers, but employees now contribute equally to the end result: shorter tenure and reduced commitment. Employees want to get what they can get, while they can get it—and then get out. Passion and pride rarely play a role in employment; few employers still inspire these emotions in their employees.

It's no wonder employees suffer from burnout and frustration. Many of us long for the ability to escape our jobs and become something else—perhaps an artist, brewer, musician, or winemaker. Envy of these jobs results from a desire to combine livelihood *and* passion. We dream of having a job that incorporates ownership, influence, and expression. Let's get beyond the titles and surroundings of our current jobs, and focus from root to harvest for inspiration in management. Let's *be the vintner*!

Chapter 1

BE THE VINTNER
(ÊTRE UN VIGNERON)

It's first thing in the morning, and as I walk out the door, the dew is settling on the leaves. I make my way through the vineyard to check the ripeness of the grapes. I look across the land and remember why I am enthusiastic each day to be a vintner. I don't mind the long hours or the effort, because at the end of the day, I have my wine to be proud of and my harvest to celebrate.

WAIT A MINUTE.... That is not my reality. I come into work and start talking to myself. *Geez, I have got to snap out of it. I am so disengaged from this position and this company. How do I get out of here? This is not what I had in mind at all. Where is the reward? How do I make an impact here? Ever since I was made a manager, I have gone from something I knew and cared about to being an overpriced babysitter stuck in a tug of war between leadership and the workforce. UGGGH!*

Through the generations, many of those who have successfully made their way to management have questioned their choice of career path. From millennials to baby boomers, they've shared many of the same emotions through different stages of their professional journeys. Maybe they are disillusioned or burned out, or maybe they are just envious of others who seem to have selected a more expressive, self-satisfying path. Maybe it is time to try to become the vintner of their workplace.

What does it mean to *be the vintner?* It means to assume the persona of a winemaker while performing your job. The word *vintner* has evolved from *wine merchant* to *winemaker*, but for our purposes, *vintner* will be synonymous with *winemaker*. *Be the vintner* will serve as the mantra of this book. As you read, you will learn about the similarities of a vintner's job to that of a manager in the workplace. A path will be provided to develop the attitude and passion of a vintner while managing your employees. After all, a vintner is someone who:

- grows the grapes

- monitors the health of the vineyard

- assures the quality of the grapes

- governs the time of harvest

- orchestrates the pressing of the grapes

- blends the juice for the wine

- samples the product

- celebrates the success of the season

So, how can you be the vintner of your workplace? By applying the same techniques with your employees that vintners do with their vines and grapes; and, most importantly, by performing your job with thirst and fervor.

It's all about attitude and vision. With the success and expansion of domestic vineyards and boutique wineries, we no longer drink wine and visualize boxes or jugs. We visualize craftsmanship, family tradition, and the sights, smells, and sounds of the vineyard and barrel room. We dream of a villa among the hills, a small tasting room in a historic town, or the fragrance of fermenting fruit and aging oak. We imagine the vintners walking their fields, checking their crops, anticipating the harvest. We see them nurturing the plants, personally involved in the winemaking experience. We flash back to movies like *Sideways, French Kiss,* or *Walk in the Clouds,* which featured romance with the land and the art of winemaking. We connect not only with the owner of the vineyard, but with their heritage, the natural process, and generations of winemaking. We envision sweat, savoring, and celebration—a labor of love. This is not a job—this is a lifestyle!

If you have visited a winery and spoken to the owners, there's a good probability you've met someone who quit a career to become a vintner. Perhaps you crave a similar opportunity. You envy the environment—the land, the people, and especially the ambiance. One vintner in California said he had been an attorney, and decided to leave his practice and join his brother in opening the vineyard. Though financially his opportunities for success were significantly less realistic, the passion and drive for the project was greater than anything he had experienced in many years of practicing law. He lost his passion, and instead of adjusting his attitude, he chose, quite literally, to *be the vintner*!

Now, let's consider reality over fantasy. A vintner's job is not easy. There are long days, significant physical demands, and elements of risk outside the vintner's control. Still, if you talk to most of them, they cannot imagine doing any other job. They are passionate about what they do, from the beginning of the process to the finished bottle of wine. They embrace the lifestyle and the intrinsic rewards that sustain their enthusiasm. They are able to realize a personal sense of accomplishment, ownership in *the* product, and a refreshing way of looking at "work."

Unfortunately, we cannot all own vineyards and produce wine. This is for many obvious (and some not-so- obvious) reasons. However, we can integrate the flavor of *being the vintner* into our management style. What we are really searching for is work that provides us with engagement and joy. Work driven by passion and creativity does not feel like work; it becomes a part of you, and provides you with purpose.

Many of us have chosen a career path, gone through years of education, and climbed the ladder to arrive at a level of competency or expertise. Reaching this level of achievement only to find ourselves yearning for something else can be disheartening. If we forfeit our current career, we lose much of the investment we have made in ourselves. Instead, consider making the effort to rediscover your passion, and even find new ways to embrace your career all over again. Victor Frankl said, *"Everything can be taken from a man but one thing: the last of the human freedoms—to choose one's attitude in any given set of circumstances, to choose one's own way."*

Join us while we tie the vintner's experience to the elements of management. The biggest challenge will be to open your mind and recreate how you **feel** about managing, and the manner in which you approach it. Try not to overthink it; relax, and be willing to look through fresh eyes. Once again, from the amazing insight of Victor Frankl: *"Between stimulus and response there is a space. In that space is our power to choose our response. In our response lies our growth and our freedom."*

Chapter 2

CHANGING REALITY
(CHANGEMENT DE RÉALITÉ)

Managers' reality can be caught up in paperwork, and it is easy to arrive at the perception that you are no longer making an impact. Additionally, coming to terms with differences of opinion and philosophy within your organization can be taxing. You try not to stress about employee complaints and leadership's demands. You want to take a deep breath: OOMMMMMM. You want to travel vicariously to "la cave" (the wine cellar). What if you could guide and encourage your employees, create a collegial relationship with your fellow managers, *and* be a part of the narrative at your workplace? Wouldn't that make managing more palatable?

Perception and reality can act as both friend and enemy. Reality consists of concrete facts and objective conditions. On the other hand, perception can be defined as those same conditions seen through an individual's personal filters. These filters include one's past, personal interests, anxieties, expectations, etc. Over time, as we familiarize ourselves with a position or company, we develop perceptions of reality. Our perception can be clouded with disappointment, frustration, and even pain. Worst of all, our perception becomes our reality. Part of *being the vintner* will require letting go of tainted perceptions and working toward an optimistic view of future reality.

It is a natural desire to want to contribute. We refer to this as *creating ownership*. How often do you use the word *ownership* at your place of work? You may refer to ownership in the case of a corporate directive or search for accountability—for example, "Who owns this process?"

In business, ownership generally reflects responsibility instead of pride. Let's make ownership represent a bond to our work. Let's create a culture in which ownership represents honor. For the vintner, the winery has personality, which reflects the individual investments of its owners and workers. Customers embrace the vintner's signature—the persona exhibited in the wine. The notion of ownership stands in direct contrast to large corporations, whose primary focus is to mass-produce widgets and create profits for faceless stakeholders. We need to redirect and highlight our pride, connection, and contribution to the organization. *Be the vintner*!

Many of us have dreamed of improving our lives in comparison with our parents' or grandparents', but we also wish to preserve the heritage and personality of the businesses of their generation. One element present in those businesses was the sense of community in the workplace. This is a key element in small businesses, both past and present. Community is created as businesses spill over into their neighborhoods, encompassing friends and family. When, in corporate America, do we take the time to uncork this fundamental? And it *is* a fundamental. If you are familiar with Maslow's **hierarchy of needs**, you are aware that socialization is a human need of significant importance. In the hierarchy, socialization is preceded only by survival and safety.

Maslow's Hierarchy of Needs

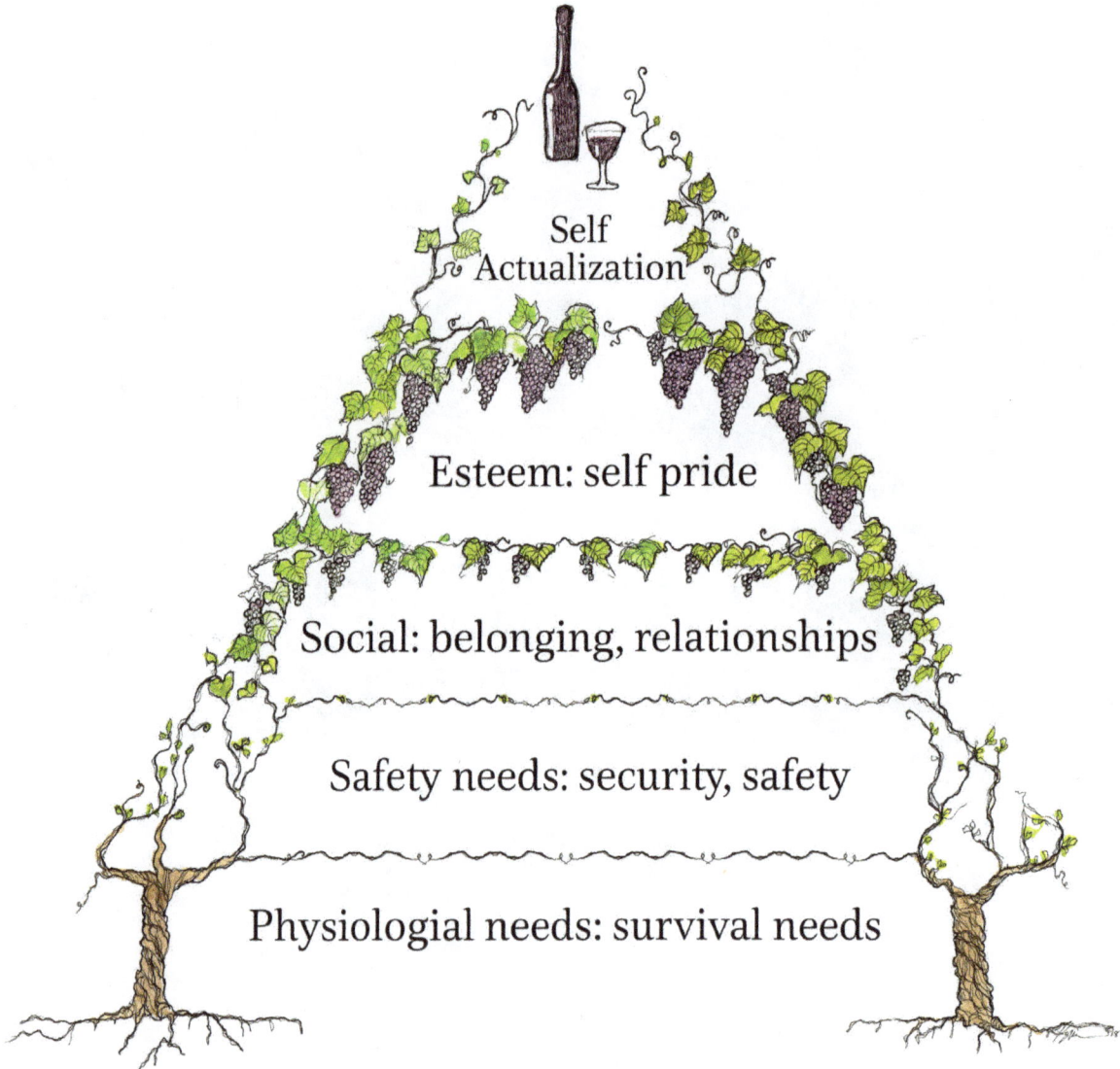

Self Actualization

Esteem: self pride

Social: belonging, relationships

Safety needs: security, safety

Physiologial needs: survival needs

Many organizations create socialization through collegial activities and teamwork. Including the greater community in the workplace only strengthens this type of social connection.

Further up on Maslow's pyramid is self-esteem, or self-actualization. We may believe that work is just a job; we work to live, we don't live to work. Since work consumes such a significant portion of our lives, if we embrace our work and employees in the same way vintners embrace their harvests and vineyards, we could achieve more satisfaction in our lives. Potentially, this could lead to a higher level of personal fulfillment while boosting our self-esteem. As we expand our emotional investment in work and embrace the people we manage, we will develop a higher sense of satisfaction.

We can allow ourselves to *be the vintner* as we manage our work teams, work projects, and daily tasks. Envision, for a moment, waking up in the morning and anticipating your day: the people, the place, the results. Let's challenge ourselves to change our perception of our work. Oh, and by the way...don't overthink it, and DO NOT take yourself too seriously. Travel vicariously to the hills of Tuscany or the vineyards of Sonoma, create a new language in the workplace/vineyard, and have some fun learning new perspectives in management.

Imagine walking through the door in the morning as the chatter is settling down in the cubicles. You make your way through the desks to check the tone of the team, look across the room, and remember why you are enthusiastic each day to be a manager. You don't mind the long hours or the effort, because at the end of the day, you have your team to be proud of and your product to celebrate as the vintner of your workplace.

Chapter 3

GROW AND CULTIVATE
(LA POUSSE ET LA CULTURE)

For the vintner, it all starts in the field. This gives "root cause" a whole different meaning. *Be the vintner*, and start with the roots of your organization: the employees. Think about where they work and what they do. After you develop strong roots, nurture and cultivate the vine until it develops to its fullest potential.

From the industrial revolution to the development of technology, our economic goals have been to drive production and financial growth through streamlining processes and eliminating waste. In the twenty-first century, employment opportunities are changing as fast as technology. Industries morph from old to new, and few people have the opportunity to embrace this metamorphosis proactively and with confidence. Companies tend to bring in employees without proper provisions. Organizations tend to overlook their employees' need for a comprehensive orientation and/or necessary handoff and training. Additionally, organizations rarely take the time to create a sense of belonging to their company or product. In order for roots to be strong, they must be entrenched within the organization.

As a result of living in a world of technology and virtual reality, most employees crave things they can touch, feel, and experience. They long to be part of their work and part of the organization's narrative. It is time to embrace the people behind the products and services. Educate your employees about the meaning and value of their work. Let them know that they are part of something bigger. Help them create a relationship with the organization and its services or products as well as the stakeholders. Reject mass-produced, nameless products and services; instead, embrace ownership and personalization.

GROW THE GRAPES (FAIRE GRANDIR LES RAISINS)

The planting of the vine is a selection process based upon a much-coveted end product. Think of the varieties that might be created: a merlot, a rosé, a chardonnay.... In order to produce a variety, one must select the root stock, or stocks. The question is, do you want to select roots with an established history, or choose a fresh variety, new and full of possibilities? Do you want to make affordable table wine, or a fine wine that is sought after, not settled for? Once you determine the strategic position of your product and organization, you can better select the right roots (or the right people) to hire.

New stock brings exciting potential, and seasoned roots have a history of performance. Think of the selections you make with employees; they are the roots of your organization. They provide crucial support for your product or service. They are an extension of you. Complex grapes, similar to complicated employees, will take more of your time and require more attention. However, they may provide the necessary flavor to give your product the edge to stand out from the competition. Once you have determined your choice, be prepared with the proper support system to fortify your selection. A vintner would never think about preparing the soil *after* planting the vines. Proactively lay the necessary groundwork in your department for a successful employee hire.

When you are selecting employees to fill a need in your department, perform your analyses before starting your search. Consider your needs as a manager as well as those of your team and the organization as a whole. Prioritize the necessary skills, experience, knowledge, and even personality for the position. Personality is important, especially if the employee will function as part of a team. Within your team, there are roles that members fill. You should understand how a candidate will integrate with the other team members, then make the appropriate preparation to assimilate the new employee into the team. Use your intuition and emotional intelligence to maneuver through this part of the employment process. There are many available assessments that can help your effort, and that you can use as part of the screening process. These assessments can help you better understand your new employees, and better develop your approach to dealing with their integration. Consider the DISC©, Predictive Index, or various other basic assessments now available.

NURTURING THE VINEYARD (NOURRIR LE VIGNOBLE)

The selection criteria to the right have been designed to provide an opportunity for you, as a manager, to consider some of the subtler factors inherent to hiring an employee. The obvious considerations—skills, knowledge, experience, and physical capability—are easy to identify through a resume and an interview. The less obvious characteristics include maturity (not age), emotional intelligence (not IQ), personality, and adaptability. We identify these characteristics through less-conventional interview techniques involving complex, behaviorally-based, open-ended questions.

Selection Criteria

Vintner's Consideration	Employee Criteria	Factors
The age and history of the vine	The maturity and performance of the employee	What is the level of internal training and mentoring available?
The flavor palete of the grape	The personality of the employee and their emotional intelligence	How will this member "blend" into the existing team or lead a team?
Suitability to the climate	The employee's ability to work within the environment or culture of your organization	Is this a long-term member or a short-term fix? Can you sustain them?
Adaptability of the vine to weather	Employee's ability to adapt to the pace and demands of the organization	Will the employee weather the storm or consume resources?

For a better understanding of these characteristics, let's look to the vineyards. Imagine the regions of France, Germany, and Italy; their wines represent a reflection of the vines in the region, further influenced by each culture and country's culinary palate. The vines are dependent upon the climate, rainfall, soil, and temperature. Employees are living, breathing organisms. They require similar consideration and nourishment. Too often, managers prioritize their own needs and the needs of the organization, overlooking the needs of their employees. It would be ill-advised to misalign an employee with an environment or culture for which they were not suited. Imagine putting an inexperienced employee in a workplace without support and mentoring, or putting an employee from a *laissez-faire* environment into a rigorously structured organization. In both cases, you risk creating an unhappy, unmotivated individual—or, at the very least, an unproductive employee. Not only does this impact the employee, but it could exert a negative impact on other, previously satisfied employees. Integration is something that the employee and employer have to work together to implement, through communication and adaptation.

People are able to adapt outside their comfort zones and stretch, but their success and productivity may be limited when they are employed in a less-than-optimal situation. The successful matching of employee with job opportunity and organizational culture provides the best chance for survival and success. In grape varieties that can survive outside their natural growing region, the resulting crop will be a reflection of how well the vine was able to adapt. Similarly, an employee's performance will reflect management style, a specific set of job requirements, and how well the employee was able to integrate into their work environment. As vintners, it is our job to help mature and grow employees while helping them fit into the environment of the organization.

Be the vintner. What helps your vineyard thrive, not just survive? When it comes to people, ask more than what their needs are; ask what their wants and expectations are. Remember, employees have free will; grapes do not. Where your employee works, who they work with, which tasks they are assigned, which resources and support they are provided, and how much time and patience they will require—all of these things should be taken into account when hiring and supporting an employee. Once you have hired an employee, you need to move to the nurturing phase, so the employee can become a viable member of the organization.

Management Grid

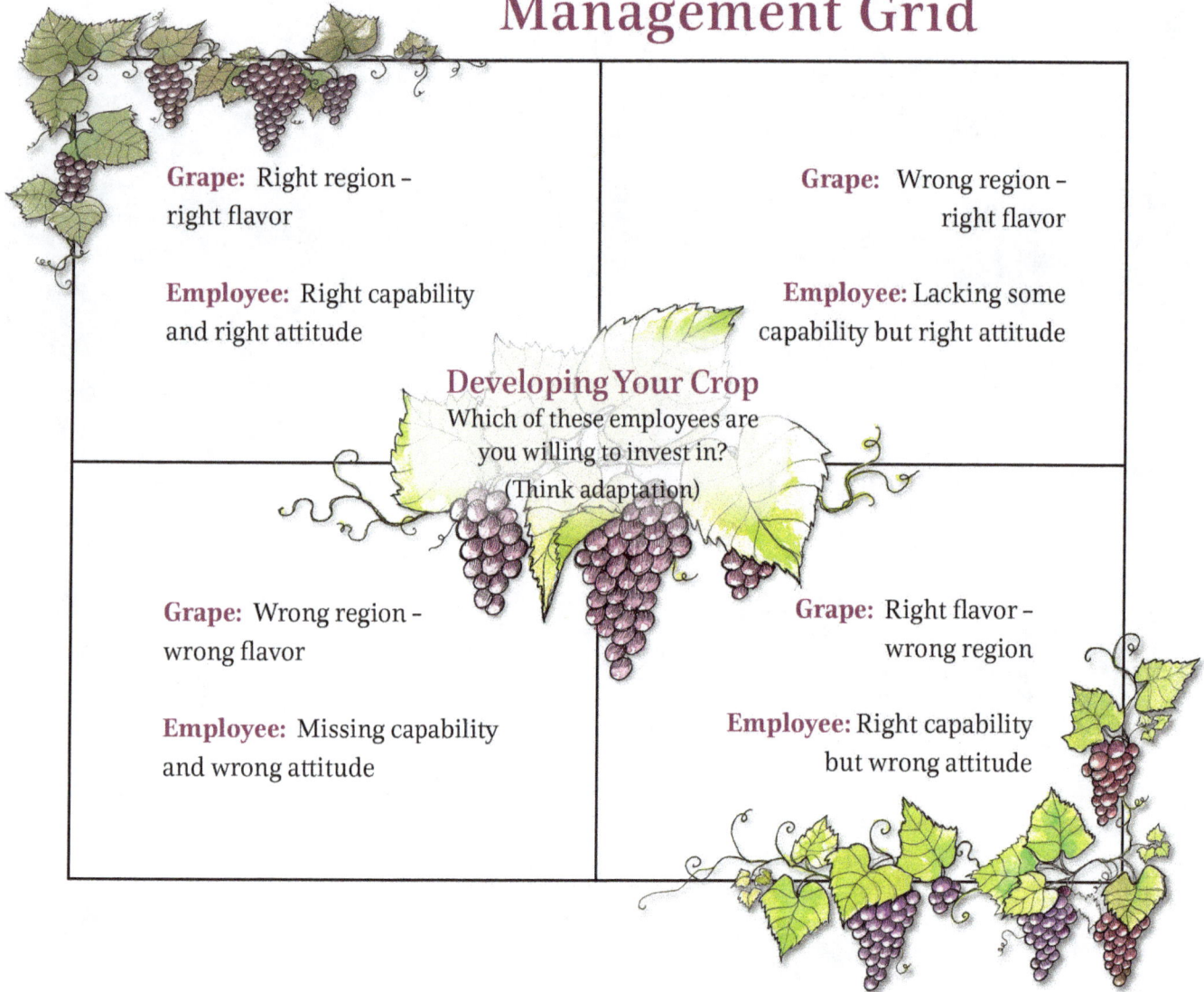

Grape: Right region – right flavor

Employee: Right capability and right attitude

Grape: Wrong region – right flavor

Employee: Lacking some capability but right attitude

Developing Your Crop
Which of these employees are you willing to invest in?
(Think adaptation)

Grape: Wrong region – wrong flavor

Employee: Missing capability and wrong attitude

Grape: Right flavor – wrong region

Employee: Right capability but wrong attitude

The management grid to the left challenges you to consider how a combination of two significant dynamics can impact the amount of effort required for success. While integrating employees into your blend, make sure that you have a good root stock worthy of your effort and investment. As the vintner of your workplace, you need to find the right flavors and capabilities in each employee. Once you determine that the flavor of a candidate blends with your organization, mature the vine (employee) for long-term growth. With employees, the right attitude–like the flavor of a grape–is something that cannot be easily changed. The act of identifying a candidate's attitude and considering their impact on your organization and team must be high-priority in your vetting process. It is often easier to train a skill than to modify a person's attitude. Matching as many other desired characteristics as possible will ensure a more successful employment outcome. A well-suited employee yields strong results.

The nurturing of the vineyard starts at the soil, and works its way up the vine and onto the trellis; it is impacted by water, the orientation of the slope, and the temperature of the sun. Growing healthy, sweet, or flavorful grapes does not just happen. It takes experience, resources, and commitment to develop a healthy, happy vineyard—and, eventually, the desired wine. Can you meet your employee's required nourishment? Employees have career goals, personal paths, and home lives. The greater the number of these elements that can be satisfied, the deeper the employee's roots will be planted. Creating this type of satisfaction and allowing employees to fulfill their potential results in dedicated, productive, long-term employees.

Be the vintner. Take your new employee, and walk them through your vineyard. Tell them about its history, discuss the last couple of harvests, and challenge them to help you improve upon the most recent release. Set expectations, and challenge them to strive for excellence as part of your team. As the vintner, you must show enthusiasm in order to grow enthusiasm! Orient employees to be engaged within the organization. This is where you make it memorable. Instill a sense of belonging to your organization's culture, product, suppliers, and customers. If you are not enthusiastic about the current elements of your organization, offer up an opportunity for your team to be part of the positive changes you hope to see. At the very least, you will need to show optimism in order to instill commitment.

Vintners must continue to pay attention to environmental impact, the accessibility of resources, and neighboring crops. Employers need to do the same. Balance your focus on the organization's needs *and* the needs of your employees. Recognize that the organization has to take priority, in many cases. At the same time, opportunities exist for taking the needs of both the employee *and* the organization into consideration, thereby creating a mutually beneficial option. Remember, employees can be the differentiating factor within your organization, giving you the edge over the competition. It is important to consider the employee, and bring their requirements to the forefront during organizational decision-making.

Driving too hard for the bottom line can cause organizations to sacrifice team members and lose the competitive advantage provided by strong, creative, valuable employees. Employees are aware when they are being sacrificed for company profits. These business strategies will generally not survive over the long term. In a competitive employment market, employees will seek out employers who value them, and leave employers who treat them as disposable.

How can we differentiate ourselves as a valued employer? Just to show how subtle differences can have a large impact, consider the Cabernet grape. This grape is grown in Fresno and in Napa; there is a five-degree temperature difference and 200 miles between them. This difference yields a significant value variance. The grape grown in Fresno sells for approximately $260 per ton, whereas the Cabernet grape grown in Napa yields as much as fifteen times that value. The difference in grape size, shape, and

flavor is not nearly significant enough to create this price variance, but the prestige of the region, the cost of the land, and the demand in this location for Cabernet grapes is phenomenal. Napa's Cabernet is one of the most expensive, in-demand wines in the region, and this has created the perfect opportunity for Napa grape growers.

How can you gain a five-degree advantage as an employer? Have an additional five-minute conversation, or send a five-sentence email offering feedback and reinforcement to your employee. These are small efforts that can yield sizeable results. Caring for and supporting an employee to a greater degree than another company or manager will set you apart. Allowing an employee to have influence within their job and area of expertise could be your five-degree difference. Show patience, even when dealing with the small, seemingly petty issues that arise among employees. Recognize that employees spend as much time with you and your company as they do with their families and friends. Help them see that their time and effort is valued. Let them realize that you appreciate whatever they are giving up in order to work for you.

Additional efforts you can make include: focusing upon improvement of your management style, creating a more desirable company culture, motivating teamwork, and providing opportunities. Thoroughly evaluate what you can offer before you hire. Make sure you represent your company honestly in your presentation. Ensure that both you and your candidate are willing to embrace common ground and overcome differences. Do not oversell or be in denial with regard to organizational reality.

How can we apply this five-degree advantage to your employee? Consider an employee available in the right location, with the skills to accomplish the right job, the right attitude and the right flavor, and the ability to offer the five-degree difference that yields more value to the organization. This same employee, without one or more of these qualities, may not be capable of providing that difference. Think of it this way: an employee with talent and enthusiasm can thrive and increase their value for the right employer, or underperform for another employer who lacks the right culture or opportunity. Detrimental factors could include location, industry, or style, resulting in failure to engage the employee in a winning fashion.

CULTIVATE (CULTIVER)

To cultivate a vineyard is to foster growth through labor and care. Managing or cultivating people is virtually the same: fostering growth through caring. Occasionally, managers may feel as if cultivating an employee is an inconvenience or necessary evil. *Be the vintner!* Like the vines in the field and the grapes on the vine, without an employee to perform a task, your organization would not produce–or you would have to perform these tasks on your own. Embrace the employee, with all of their human characteristics, as an extension of your skill, knowledge, and creativity. Employees are vital to your work and the success of your product or service. They are the grapes of your wine, and provide flavor and body to the organization. So when an employee needs attention, do not consider them an inconvenience; instead, view them as your purpose. Consider this: some of your best relationships grow out of associations with employees and coworkers. While you are tending to them, they are helping develop your management skills, emotional intelligence, and insight.

Make your workplace your vineyard. A vintner comes to work and observes the vineyard, oversees the crop, monitors the weather, and makes sure the vines are weeded, fertilized, and watered. *Be the vintner;* start your day in the same way. Walk your department, observe your employees, and pay attention to the details. Does Mary look rested? Are there new pictures on Joe's desk? Do these employees look healthy and productive? Do they have the right tools and environment for success? Who is missing today (physically or mentally)? If something is lacking, don't let your employees die on the vine. Bring a little warmth, a little sunlight (say good morning, and ask if they need assistance.) Sprinkle a bit of water (offer advice and communicate.) Make sure they have the nutrients for growth (train, mentor, and provide positive reinforcement). Change your attitude about the human element in the workplace. Recognize the importance of managing and nurturing your team.

THE CROP (LA RÉCOLTE)

Beyond the individual there is the team. They represent your crop.

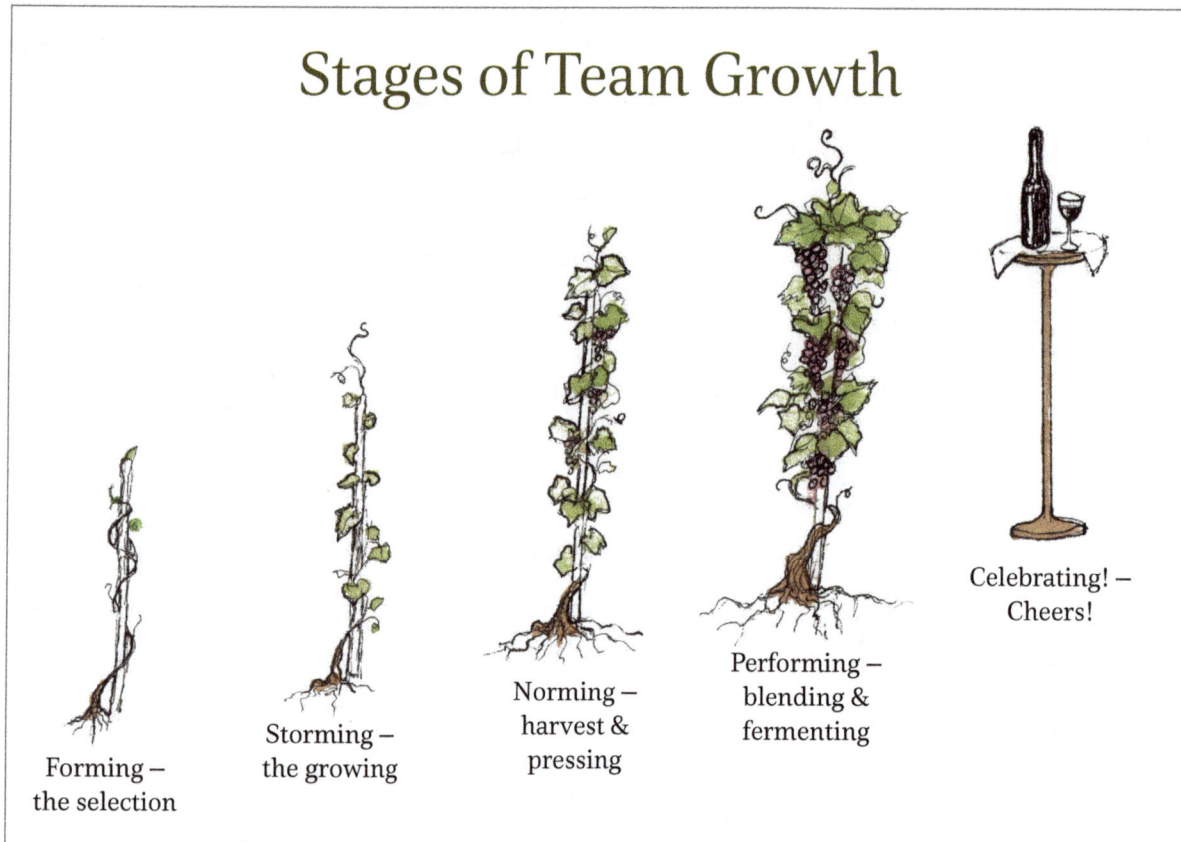

Stages of Team Growth

Forming – the selection

Storming – the growing

Norming – harvest & pressing

Performing – blending & fermenting

Celebrating! – Cheers!

Be the vintner! Winemaking has several stages, much like the phases of team-building. Let's compare.

Forming: The formation of a new vineyard involves the selection and planting of the vines. This stage requires lots of nurturing, observation, and hands-on involvement to assure survival of the plants.

- With employees, the newly-formed team is exploring issues, familiarizing themselves with their job responsibilities, and adjusting to their new environment through many informal conversations. For the manager, like the vintner, now is the time to stay focused on the team: reinforcing desired behaviors and communications and discouraging unhealthy habits.

Storming: The growing process. Now that the vines are in the field, it is time to maintain good health. Watch for signs of pests, fungus, and blight. Make sure to add the necessary nutrients to encourage growth.

- Your team is established, and is now vying for roles. There will be conflict regarding the development of processes and procedures. It is your job to make sure it's healthy conflict: professional, not personal. Facilitate fair play among team members. Allow the team to work through their challenges, but referee from the sidelines to make sure that less-assertive members build confidence and hold their own.

Norming: With a mature crop, it is time to harvest and press. If the vintners have done their job and Mother Nature has been on their side, the vines are strong and the fruit has ripened. The grapes have reached their anticipated flavor.

🍇 Check the readiness of your team members. Are they prepared to fulfill the role you intended for them? Will they provide the necessary contributions? If not, press a bit, and finesse. While pressing, do not overstress; allow the team to remain motivated and confident.

Performing: The blending and aging process. Combine the flavors of the juice you have extracted, and let it age to perfection. Stay close, and observe the process. Fine wine is the result of planning and patience.

🍇 Your team members have settled into appropriate and productive roles within the group. They are maturing their communication techniques and resolving challenges. Help them develop team norms and values. If they seem imbalanced, (a bit too much tannin or sugar), then do more blending. Pull back on the delegation of one employee, and press a bit more on another. If you have done your job right and luck is on your side, you can relax and let them perform (ferment). Continue to walk the room and observe the process, and provide timely feedback.

Adjourning: A tasting and celebrating process. Taste your outcome, celebrate your success, share your product, and learn from the experience.

🍇 Take a look at the work accomplished. Is it all you anticipated? If not, re-evaluate your blend. If it is, CELEBRATE! Acknowledge success, and have a time of CHEER!

In general, pay attention to the influences impacting your team. When a fungus or pest causes blight to the crop, a vintner springs into action. Focus on the need of the crop, and cure the ill. Triage the most destructive element first, and take immediate and permanent action to isolate as much of the disease as possible. Imagine how much healthier your workplace would be if you approached employee issues the way a vintner cares for the vineyard. When you procrastinate in the resolution of employee issues, small matters become big complications. Time spent overanalyzing and suffering through impending discipline or corrective action creates unnecessary stress. Procrastination on your part may also be perceived by members of your team as inaction.

The key is timing:

- don't dwell

- react, repair, or replace

- take the necessary action!

- share your observations and feedback in real time

A common misconception among managers is that their team accepts the manager's priorities. When remedying a workplace problem takes longer than necessary, it has a lasting impact on surrounding and supporting employees. When a manager reacts in a timely manner and does the right things, they replace perceived weakness with respect and admiration. Stress and worry over employee discipline is generally more burdensome than the action itself. A vintner cannot ignore pests or disease. Mother Nature is cruel to vintners who do not constantly care for their vineyards. As a manager, it is important that you regularly:

- assign projects

- document behavior

- train skills

- resolve conflict

Prioritize the necessary employee action, then address it and check the tasks off your list. Ignoring and avoiding employee challenges will interfere with your ability to lead. *Be the vintner*; be the proactive leader for your team. Get past the challenge, then recharge and focus on the positive. Let your newfound energy "be the sun, the nutrients, or the fertilizer," whatever suits the situation.

THE VINEYARD (LE VIGNOBLE)

Maintain a clean, comfortable, well-designed vineyard. Be the vintner: incorporate creative elements into your workplace. Even a dusty, dingy warehouse can include elements of lightness, motivation, and inspiration. Obviously, vineyards and wineries have visual advantages over many worksites...but think outside the box. How can you bring positive or natural elements into your workspace? This can be done with color, sound, plants, pictures, posters, or banners. Do not make expense a hurdle; make it a challenge. Create a vision, and make it a team priority. Let it materialize. Too often, we underestimate our own or our team's ability to transform a workplace on a budget. When the project provides creative expression and generates personal reward, employees become activated. The environment gives the employees a sense of ownership and personal pride. Enlist your team's help, and empower them!

Beyond appearance, consider how behavior impacts the team's attitude and perception. Don't stay hunkered down at your office or desk. *Be the vintner* of your team: walk, talk, share, and engage. Move around, and set aside more face time with your employees. Engage and create a working relationship. Help your team truly know their product, their organization, and you. Incorporate transparency into your daily communications. You may be familiar with the song "I Heard It Through the Grapevine." How many times does the rumor mill outdo honest, planned organizational communication? You can eliminate stress on your team and yourself by paying attention to the flow of communication. Your vineyard needs direct sunlight and rain. Remember, you are not raising mushrooms—you know, kept in the dark and fed manure! Communication

should occur weekly or daily. Information will provide your employees with the confidence of knowing where they and the organization are headed.

How many vineyards do you see cloaked in darkness? Visualize the difference between a vintner and a mad scientist. Imagine one walking the land, roaming the casks and the tasting room; and the other behind a locked door, developing the latest scary concoctions to abolish the world. If it is not visible, IT IS SCARY! Perception becomes reality to the recipient. When team members are aware of the reality, or even the challenges of an organization or department, they can respond in an appropriate fashion and assist in problem-solving or preparation. Do not overprotect employees; communicate so they can play a role in their workplace destiny. This is called empowerment...which results in employee engagement!

Just as a vintner would provide nutrition to the vines, you must provide information in the workplace. Just as a weatherperson helps a vintner prepare for unsettling weather conditions, a manager needs to prepare their team for changes in organizational climate. What would happen if a vintner were unaware of an impending drought or frost? The crop would be damaged. Even a bumper crop year could become a loss if a team lacks preparation. You can never have so many resources that waste is acceptable. Communication is better, even though knowledge can, at times, create fear. Reinforcing ignorance—and, ultimately, creating mistrust—comes at a heavier price. Employees want to stand for something meaningful; having influence over their own fate gives them purpose. Even when times are tough within your organization, allow your employees the knowledge necessary to participate in organizational outcomes.

Use both informal and formal channels of communication to share knowledge. Every day can be an opportunity for teambuilding and relationship-deepening. Create workplace events and trainings. See the interrelated results of your actions and interactions. When you educate, you can empower and advance employees. When you promote from within, you motivate employees to work harder and smarter. This is your impact or impression upon your team and organization. You can influence the final product by *being the vintner*. Remember the word *ownership*; allow your employees to exercise ownership within their work.

Chapter 4

HARVEST AND PRESS
(LA RÉCOLTE ET LE FOULAGE)

HARVEST (RÉCOLTER)

For the vintner, to harvest is to bring the fruit out of the vineyards and into the winery; the quality of the grapes will dictate the quality of the wine. The time of harvest is decided primarily by the ripeness of the grapes and the intended wine as determined by the vintner. The harvesting of wine grapes is one of the most essential steps in the process of winemaking.

Be the vintner. Harvest early in the morning; bring the fruit in before the sun touches the clusters. Hot fruit, or fruit that has been handled roughly, will produce a more volatile acidity and spontaneous fermentation. With employees, whether it is early in the day or early in their career, timing is important. The scheduling of meetings, trainings, employee reviews, and feedback should be based upon order of importance. Is the matter critical, requiring you to catch the employee fresh, first thing in the morning? Or is it of lower priority, which would allow for a working lunch or afternoon appointment with a less-focused, more fatigued employee? Remember, the timing of workday activities impacts participation, information retention—and, sometimes, results.

To paraphrase Gina Gallo in her video on the subject, while gearing up for harvest, we spend a lot of time in vineyard. We reflect upon the last season and the season before. There is a lot of planning, as well; but once the harvest begins, that plan may get thrown out the window. During the harvest, it's like being on call. You never know what is going to happen. You get to watch the evolution of the wine.

Managers check the readiness of their team members and confirm their ability to fulfill their roles. With your communication and strategy in place, plan for the necessary production. If you find that your team has not matured to the required level, step up their training and mentoring, and enlist the support of seasoned employees to aid your effort.

Recognize that your results are greater than one person. It is still vital to stay close to your process and stay involved at all levels with your employees. Don't forget—empowerment is not a license to disengage from the management and support of your team. Too often, managers and leaders step away from their teams—too soon, too long, and too frequently. Be close, be approachable, and take ownership. *Be the vintner*!

Gina Gallo also commented that what is really enjoyable about harvest time is the camaraderie, the energy of the team: staying on the same page, very focused, moving forward. It takes a lot of us to create success. The challenging side is the promises you make to yourself. The grapes change, the season changes, and Mother Nature changes, but it is about going in there and trying to create the best possible wine. Harvest time is two months out of the year, and then, the wine is alive. The closer the winemaker stays to the product, the more interesting and creative wine they can bring to the consumer.

Every day, *be the vintner* and aim for the harvest. Imagine seeing the first buds on the vine, the small pea-shaped grapes forming in the spring, and the vines thriving in the warmth of summer. The grapes evolve into a deep purple or gold of ripeness. Think of your employees in the same way. See the candidate for an interview, then anticipate their first day on the job. Nurture them through the orientation process,

continue to stay close, and encourage them through the process of their organizational integration. If you see an employee with a quizzical look on their face struggling to find the break room and fearful to ask questions in meetings, you can then watch that same employee progress to become a viable team member—challenging their colleagues, and not just asking questions, but making recommendations, as well. This should provide you with a sense of pride, for growing an employee is no easy task; it takes patience, skill, and emotional intelligence. Your job is not done yet! Stay close to the wine. Continue to create the opportunities your employees thirst for. Provide learning and experiences through delegation (let them participate in the harvest). This is the only way an employee can become part of the blend—by contributing to the flavor of your organization.

Employees, like grapes, mature at different paces. Some peak early in their tenure, and others take time to develop to their full potential. Remaining aware of their "ripeness" (the readiness of your employees) is subtle, but vital to any manager's success.

- Has this employee acclimated to the workplace and their team?

- Do they have confidence in their assignment?

- Is their confidence warranted?

- When delegating to them, how much oversight is necessary?

- If you were the vintner, when would you assess the vine's stability?

- When should you reduce the amount of nurturing?

Once the vines are stable and the watering system is reliable, it's time to let them grow! Consider empowering your employees once they are familiar with the processes and are working well as a team.

Whether you are watching the growth of the vines and the ripeness of the grapes or watching the evolution of the team and the maturing of the employees, vintner-managers have the responsibility to develop the qualities within their team to meet the production needs of the organization. In employment, this occurs through training, mentoring, delegating, and empowering. You start with the site, by showing pride and caring for your facility and tools. Then you move to the culture: how you and the organization project your image, and how your employees are treated. Once your site and culture are solid, move to your people and your product or service. Just remember, you cannot grow your position without developing sturdy roots around you.

PRESS (FOULER)

Many times, the grapes are allowed to rest following the harvest. They are destemmed, then allowed to release the "free run" juice from the grape. This occurs by the weight of their own grape berries and clusters. While this is high-quality juice, there is still more juice remaining in the grapes. Most wines are made from both free-run juice and pressed juice.

Be the vintner! Know your employees. Many employees are driven and work flows freely from them, while other employees require a bit more "pressing." For those who are self-starters and overachievers, let them provide you with their free-run

juice. Provide guidance and feedback, show appreciation, and acknowledge their accomplishments. Taking a high-achieving employee for granted is a common, but dangerous, practice. Be sure not to ignore your achievers. Continue to challenge them, keeping them stimulated and rewarded.

Then there are those who need pressing. Managers delegate, challenge, and extract work from employees in many different ways. You have to press enough to motivate, but not so much that you damage morale or overstress. Develop the emotional intelligence to know when to apply just the right pressure, at just the right time, to just the right individual or combination of employees.

Your goal is to accomplish this task without wasting resources or understaffing the effort. The degree of pressing is determined by the demands of the goals and the quality of the output. Your style of management will determine how and when you choose to press employees. Like a fine vintner with years of experience, finesse the juice from the grapes and deliver the best product to start the fermentation process. A well-managed team effort results in sweet success!

Chapter 5

BLENDING AND AGING
(LE MÉLANGE ET LE VIEILLISSEMENT)

BLENDING (LE MÉLANGE)

Professional winemakers are the first to admit that few standalone grapes have the characteristics of a flawless wine. Blending allows the vintner to pick the finest characteristics of two or more grapes and join them together for flavor perfection. This is a centuries-old technique. It is all about running tests, comparing flavors, and finding just the right ratios before you commit to the final blend. Your ultimate goal is to create something that suits your taste and produces the best final product for your customer.

Certainly, there are grapes that stand on their own, and there is no reason to mess with excellence. However, when wines are a bit thin, a little too sweet, or simply lacking in dimension, this is where blending comes into play. The possibilities for blending are endless, limited only by the grapes selected.

Recognizing that most wines benefit from blending, there are good and bad reasons to blend. Similarly, there are good and bad reasons to blend employees in the context of a team or project.

Reasons to blend:

- 🍷 The pursuit of balance: with wines, a happy partnership of fruit, tannin, color, and (sometimes) oak makes great wines soar and lesser wines fall flat.

  - *Be the vintner! Assess your employees when it is time to add resources to your group. Think of what is missing from your current mix. In what areas involving skills, personality, or knowledge is the team weak? Are there natural leaders who could be your second in command (succession planning), or do you need to add leadership? Do you need more consistency and stability on the team? Would your team benefit from an innovator to spike the creativity? Think about all of the facets of your team, and make a list of missing elements to create the perfect blend. Search for candidates with the desired characteristics, and select the one(s) who will best complement you and your team's needs.*

- 🍷 The pursuit of added complexity: create a variety of flavors and aromas, something to stimulate every part of your taste buds, a wine with plenty of character at the start and something left for the finish.

  - *Be the vintner. A good manager knows that not everyone has to share the manager's opinion. There is strength in diversity; it increases creativity and opportunities for success. Do you have enough diversity in your team to create healthy conflict and challenge the status quo? If everyone on a team acts and thinks like the manager, the result can lack complexity. The team can end up with too narrow a vision, and can miss obvious opportunities and make mistakes. Healthy debates result from blending.*

🍇 Do not blend to improve bad wine; a small amount of bad wine should not be blended with good wine. When you blend the bad with the good, you are left with a lesser-quality product. This is very similar to employee blends. Evaluate your team, and repair or replace problem employees.

As in the blending of grapes, realizing the potential of collaboration between different teams and team members is a sign of confidence and experience in management. All successful companies and teams, no matter how skilled or diverse, perform certain tasks well, and other tasks not so well. By enlisting team members, external teams, or companies, you can focus on what you do best and expose the existing team to new strategies for accomplishing goals.

Be the vintner. With wine, it is not always smooth at first taste. Sometimes, the flavor is too acidic. Similarly, there may be friction within the team. This is where good managers insert themselves and help members mature and appreciate each other for the value they bring. Help your team members look past the obvious differences of new members and better understand the value of diversity.

Sometimes, we make a poor selection. It is our job, then, to save the wine, as noted in our discussion on growing and nurturing. Take ownership in the mentoring, pressing, and blending of your team. After you have put forward your best effort, be willing to take responsibility and remove any resource that does not add to the desired fullness

and flavor. Be objective; it should not be personal preference, but a professional assessment. Be effective and decisive, and repair or remove what does not work in a timely manner.

Blending can leave you with a wine that is flat, or one that is tastier than a single grape can produce. The only way to know for sure if a blend will work is to try it.

With employees, as you continue to blend your team, think of the makeup of a high-performing team. It requires trust, communication, shared goals, internal and external support, commitment, relevant skills, and leadership. A manager needs to be a good leader. They also need the appropriate skills and the wherewithal to hire the right people with those skills. As a manager, you will need to continue to lobby for external support, and reinforce the team's collaborative effort and mutual support. Communication is indispensable, and a primary responsibility of the manager and vintners. Trust is earned over time through honest communication and a stable team relationship.

Be the vintner! Consider these steps for blending your team:

1. Recruit using several tasters; multiple palates are always better than one. (Include other members of your organization in your recruiting/interviewing.)

2. Take time to identify the flavors. Don't just rate them "good" or "bad." (Break down the advantages and disadvantages of a potential team member, and really listen to both sides of the discussion.) Have a comprehensive discussion about the candidates. Apply what you learn from interviewing one candidate to your next interview.

3. Keep careful track, and keep notes on what the tasters find in each. There is bound to be too much information to keep in your head, so take copious notes, reviewing them with your selection team. Learning from your wins and your misses will help you to make future improvements. Do a thorough evaluation prior to deciding your next move.

AGING (LE VIEILLISSEMENT)

Aging may improve the quality of wine. The recommended aging time is influenced by many factors, including grape variety, vintage, wine region, and winemaking style. The quality of an aged wine varies significantly from bottle to bottle. The outcome depends upon the conditions under which the wine is stored, and the condition of the bottle and cork. It is said that there are good old bottles. This creates a mystique around the aging of wine.

Most employees will continue to develop well into their career. During their tenure, employees gain knowledge, experience, history, and relationships. More often than not, these traits add value to performance. There is unmatched value in an employee with actual firsthand experience. They have gained confidence and the ability to quickly pull from past experience and perform. Generally speaking, if a good environment, positive leadership, and good management exist, loyalty and longer tenure will come naturally. On the other hand, do not be afraid of what we call "good turnover." It is healthy to have some change in organizations, and to gain new perspectives. Avoid getting stale and losing pace with your industry and market. If you lose a team member to a growth opportunity, wish them well. Take advantage of this opportunity to further add to your blend.

Chapter 6

CELEBRATE: CHEERS!
(CÉLÉBRATION, À LA VÔTRE!)

Celebration? If this seems like a frivolous chapter to you, stop yourself and take a moment to fully embrace *being the vintner*. Recognize that celebrations unite people and communities. Celebrating as a group generates a sense of belonging, and can transform your employees' outlook. It is an expression of gratitude for service and accomplishments. Why wouldn't you celebrate? Why wouldn't you appreciate and reflect upon the achievements of the people who produce for you?

We speak of employee engagement...then we ask employees to put their heads down and grind it out without so much as a look back or a moment to reflect. Change your thinking. *Be the vintner!* Connect the celebration to the work; connect to the customer and to future opportunities. Remember, employees are free agents; continue to find ways to give them a reason to want to work for you.

Celebrations provide the opportunity to honor significant events. They can also function as rites of passage, or recognition of progression to a certain stage of development. Even when performance has been imperfect, celebrations can help us bounce back more quickly from adversity.

The Three Glories (Les Trois Glorieuses) is an elaborate example of a wine celebration. It is an annual auction and celebration that takes place in Beaune, France. In November, winemakers taste several wines at the Hospice de Beaune's winery barrel room. Each member of the tasting groups takes detailed notes on their rating sheet as the winemaking team assesses the potential of each wine. (This is similar to the type of assessment done when recruiting a new employee.)

At the 150th Les Trois Glorieuses, the entire community participates in the celebration. On Friday night, friends and clients gather for the first dinner. The setting is a casual and relaxed, with light conversation, wine tasting, and laughter consuming the evening.

On Saturday at noon, a friendly lunch is served at an eighteenth-century estate. A welcoming speech is given by the CEO of Albert Bichot. The room breaks into a cheery rendition of the traditional Burgundy song, "Ban Bourguignon." This is a drinking song (chanson à boire) that is generally sung when large groups of people are present at the end of a meal, to foster the consumption of wine. Such singing is traditional in the wine culture of France. The simple words *la la la la la la la lalère* are repeated five or more times. The song is simple and joyous. The addition of clapping and hand gestures makes the occasion even more festive. Lunch is followed by an extensive tasting of wines from several vintages.

On Saturday afternoon, the streets of Beaune come alive, making this weekend a popular, family-oriented party. An annual half-marathon begins, followed by a bottle-opening competition. Town folk in historic costumes perform folk dances, and bands march through town. On Saturday night, a gala dinner for friends and clients takes place.

On Sunday morning, a team helps future buyers make their final choices during a last tasting at the winery. The buyers' bids are collected, and one last meal is served before the auction takes place. Passion and enthusiasm for the wine is apparent among the participants and providers. Finally, the Hospice de Beaune auction begins. Burgundy fans from all over the world, including media, gather outside.

A French actor auctions the first barrel, with the proceeds going to a charity. Rounds of applause for a record-breaking price of $400,000 euros for this barrel! The gavel strikes, and the primary auction starts with tremendous intensity. The results: 700 barrels sold for 4.5 million euros. Albert Bichot is once again the number-one buyer, and receives congratulations. The last dinner is shared at Albert Bichot's. Genuine caring is shown as the guests leave the dinner with a farewell toast.

On Monday at noon, the end of The Three Glories wraps up at the famous Paulée de Meursault. The lunch is a bittersweet time, signifying the end of a magnificent event. The notion of this meal is easy; each guest brings a bottle of their choice to share with other guests. It would not be a wrap-up without a song, which is begun by a line of men in chef's aprons. Down the long tables, guests begin singing and clapping to the music. The true emotion of the event can be appreciated by watching the YouTube video "The Weekend of Celebration in Beaune Burgundy." The video draws you in, and makes you want to be there as a part of the experience.

Though this event is grander than most, let's summarize the elements that make it such a comprehensive celebration:

- celebrates the completion of a product or service

- involves the community

- supports charity

- creates a festive and memorable occasion (by including songs, chants, and toasts)

- creates a social environment

- the event ties back to previous accomplishments

Don't be intimidated by the grandeur of the celebration in Beaune. At the other end of the spectrum, here's an example of a small but memorable celebration. When I was growing up, our family raced sailboats. One of the boat captains had a practice of bringing Oreo cookies to every race. They were known as "victory Oreos," and were shared following the race in celebration of the win. Though this was a small and inexpensive gesture, there is little I remember about those races except the victory Oreos. This memory has survived forty years with our entire family. They were hailed as a symbol of success, a reward for a job well done! To earn not just an Oreo, but a victory Oreo, was delightful.

Be the vintner! Recognize that something as small as leaving fifteen minutes early on a Friday with a high five at the door leaves employees feeling good. It fortifies the attitude you want every employee to show up with on Monday morning. The practice leads to a positive work environment, appreciation, and a sense of community. On the other hand, leaders who leave before their team every Friday leave employees feeling the exact opposite. Employees go home feeling disconnected and resentful of the "special privileges" of their manager, and go into the weekend feeling discouraged and unappreciated. This attitude might be the last thought they have on Friday evening, and the first one that surfaces again on Monday morning.

Think of the comments of Gina Gallo: "The best part of the harvest is the camaraderie and the energy of the team." Deem every day an opportunity to build team spirit. Remember in the first chapter, when we mentioned not taking yourself too seriously? This is a challenge for many managers. They want to reward their teams, but they overthink it. Many managers worry about their reward going unappreciated. If you are struggling with this, select a few influential members of the team and ask their opinion. If your idea incorporates one of these things, it will generally be well-received:

1. a personal effort or touch

2. an uncommon benefit (even a small one, i.e., a parking space, minutes off, food, or a gift)

3. positive feedback, accolades, or gratitude

Ideas and celebrations are only corny or cheesy if they are presented that way. Challenge yourself and your team to loosen up and have fun with this. Your team players will be on board with you. Remember, you are the vintner! Consider developing a team motto, mantra, or song, like the bell being rung at Trader Joe's or the jokes told by the flight attendants on Southwest Airlines. Enlist employees to help create their own celebrations that can be personalized within the workplace. If budgets are tight, replace your holiday party or company picnic with a "results event."

Remember Maslow's Theory from Chapter One? Humans strive for socialization and self-esteem. Inviting the team to participate in a "results event" enhances socialization, community, and memories. It builds self-esteem by acknowledging and reminding the employees of their personal contribution to the finished product/service. When appropriate, call out individual and team efforts that led to the end result. You can create a connection by including vendors, customers, and members of the community. If done well, the event will remain in the minds of employees, and anticipation of the next event will motivate them further.

Invite customers to provide positive feedback and perhaps include them in the celebration, when appropriate. Ask suppliers to share their stories and contribute to your event. Create opportunities to include employees' families to share in the results. Acknowledge the sacrifices employees' families make when they support their family members' contributions to organizational success. How many missed children's performances, anniversaries, or birthdays did it take to complete your product or service? Let them celebrate their accomplishments and relationship with their employer with family and community.

Make it socially responsible; involve a nonprofit or cause. Pick a charity, and find a way to share the success by making a physical, financial, or intellectual contribution. Create a win-win situation for the company and the charity.

Don't get caught up in excuses (can't afford it, don't have the time, it is not a priority). An event is one of the cheapest public-relationship and loyalty builders an organization can craft: celebration, employee benefit, social responsibility, and advertisement all rolled into one.

In business, even though we talk about celebrating, wins, and teambuilding, oftentimes it becomes the last priority and the first budget cut. *Be the vintner!* For a vintner, this is part of the business. Share the results of your labor, unveil it to the public, and invite your community to the harvest and the toast. Create community and start your own traditions. Your employees have earned it, and deserve it. And by the way, so have you. CHEERS!

Embrace your day—enjoy your people, and promote ownership of your product or service. Leave your mark by *being the vintner*.

Remember each chapter:

Grow and Cultivate—make your selections and nurture your team; Watch their readiness and help them adapt. Challenge yourself to learn what helps your vineyard thrive. Make your workplace your vineyard; keep it clean comfortable and well designed.

Harvest and Press—mentor and mature your employees, then delegate and empower them. Press and finesse work from your team as needed. Show enthusiasm to differentiate yourself as a valued manager. Lead; do not step away from your team too soon, too long or too frequently. Be close and be approachable. Don't dwell, react, repair, replace.

Blend and Age— blend the team and develop their rhythm, then build tenure;

Celebrate—Share the successes and reinforce loyalty in your team.

Most importantly, *be the vintner* in your workplace!

NOTES

BOOKS

PAGE 8:

Viktor Frankl, *Man's Search for Meaning*
(Boston: Beacon Press, 1946).

PAGE 14

Maslow, A.H. "A Theory of Human Motivation,"
Psychological Review 50, no, 4 (1943): pp.370-396.

PAGE 42

B. Tuckman, "Developmental Sequence in Small Groups,"
Psychological Bulletin 63, no. 6 (1965): pp.384-399.

VIDEO

Page 58

The Press Democrat, "Harvest with Gina Gallo." YouTube, September 23, 2009, www.youtube.com/watch?v=8QbQYJgAe6A&feature=youtu.be.

Page 82

Hospices Beaune, "A Weekend of Wine Celebration in Beaune, Burgundy, November 2010." YouTube, September 12, 2011, www.youtube.com/watch?v=vLvJDxN62gY.

SPECIAL THANKS:

Carrie & Earl Sullivan and the team at Telaya Wine Company

Cover and Interior design: Darlene Swanson - Van-garde Imagery

Artwork: Karen Bagnard – More than Mermaids

Photo edits and post-processing: Sara Clark Design + Photography

www.ingramcontent.com/pod-product-compliance
Lightning Source LLC
Chambersburg PA
CBHW050243220326
41598CB00048B/7493